All Aboard!

Trains and Texas
Brad Herzog

Contents

Rigby

A Harcourt Achieve Imprint

www.Rigby.com
1-800-531-5015

-Introduction: The Texas Express

All aboard and welcome to the Texas Express! I'm Marino T. Caboose, your conductor and engineer. Find yourself a seat by the window because we're about to begin an exciting ride on the rails. We won't just be speeding across the Lone Star State. We'll also be traveling back to the past to see how the railroad affected this part of the country. Get ready to steam ahead on a journey through Texas, technology, and time. The Texas Express is leaving the station. . . .

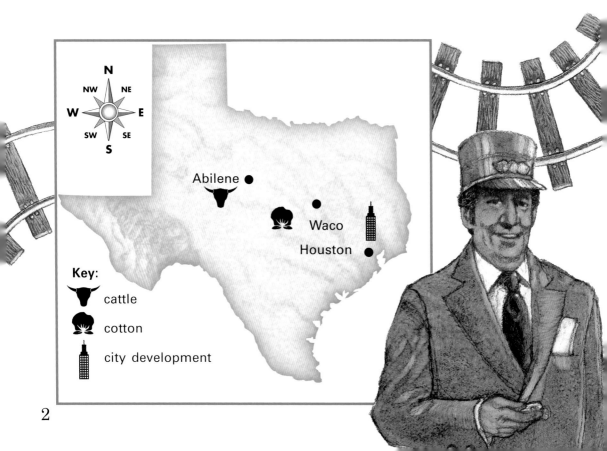

N
NW   NE
W   E
SW   SE
S

Abilene ●

Waco ●

Houston ●

Key:

🐂 cattle

🌸 cotton

🏙 city development

Progress in science and technology helped people in the United States create everything from movies to railroads.

As you are about to find out, in addition to helping people and places, scientific and technological inventions like the railroad can actually change places, too. For example, moving pictures were invented in New Jersey in 1889. About 20 years later, filmmakers began making movies in a small California town called Hollywood. As people began getting great movie jobs in Hollywood, many others decided to move there. Soon the small town of Hollywood became a big city. We're about to see how the railroad had a similar effect on another part of the country.

1 The Railroad Age

The first steam engines were built in England, yet the United States—with its wide open spaces—had a much greater need for railroads. But first the people of the United States had to overcome their disbelief that railroad technology could work. In 1826 a man named John Stevens became the "Father of American Railroads" by operating the first train engine built and run on rails in the United States. He ran it around a small, circular track in his yard!

People had many ways to get around before railroads were built. Railroads, however, quickly grew popular because they were faster and more dependable.

Before the development of trains, people in the United States walked, rode horses, took boats, or traveled in stagecoaches. When it was discovered that trains could be used to move people and goods over long distances in a much shorter time, the railroads began to grow. In 1830 there were only 23 miles of track in the United States. Twenty years later, there were more than 9,000 miles. By 1916 the number had reached a peak of 254,000 miles. The "Iron Horse," as the steam engine was called, was making tracks across America.

Locomotives like this one gradually became a common sight across the United States.

The railroad was very important to the growth of the United States. During the 1840s and 1850s, the nation's railroads continued to expand. In the early 1860s, railroads moved supplies and soldiers for both the North and the South during the American Civil War. By the later 1860s, the United States stretched from the Atlantic Ocean to the Pacific Ocean, and plans were made to lay tracks from coast to coast. There would soon be a railroad that would span the continent of North America: a transcontinental railroad.

The Growth of the Union Pacific Railroad: 1865–1869

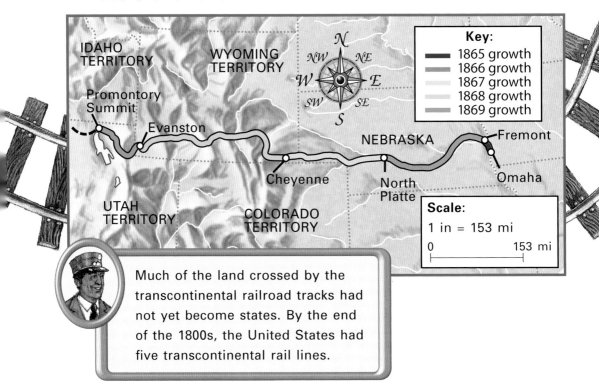

Key:	
▬	1865 growth
▬	1866 growth
▬	1867 growth
▬	1868 growth
▬	1869 growth

Scale:
1 in = 153 mi
0   153 mi

Much of the land crossed by the transcontinental railroad tracks had not yet become states. By the end of the 1800s, the United States had five transcontinental rail lines.

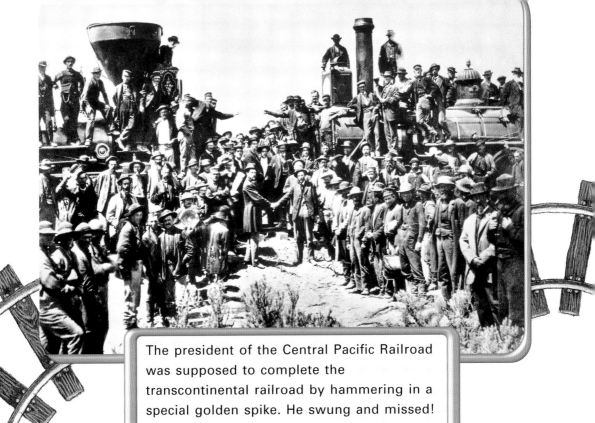

The president of the Central Pacific Railroad was supposed to complete the transcontinental railroad by hammering in a special golden spike. He swung and missed!

One railroad, the Union Pacific, laid tracks going west from the end of a railroad line in Nebraska. At the same time, the Central Pacific Railroad built tracks going east from California. For several years thousands of workers toiled, laying nearly 1,800 miles of track. Finally on May 10, 1869, the two lines met in the middle of the Utah desert at a place called Promontory Summit. Traveling across the country, which had been a journey of several months by wagon, now took only about a week.

2 First Stop . . . Houston!

Unlike many other parts of the United States, the settlement of Texas had been slow. The state's rivers were difficult to cross, and its roads were scarce and poorly maintained. However, because Texas offered more than 250,000 square miles of land and opportunity, trains and the Lone Star State were a perfect match. And Houston was where the Texas railroad adventure began.

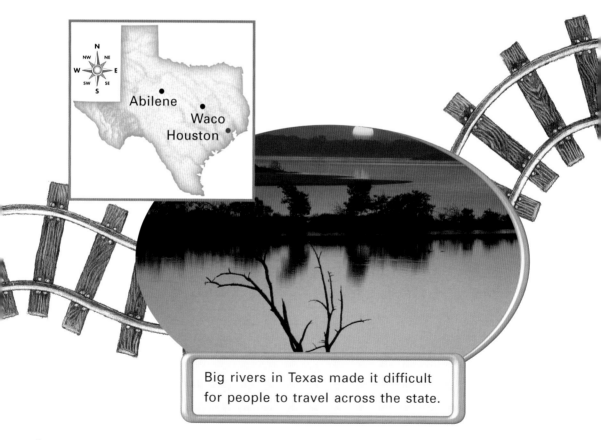

Big rivers in Texas made it difficult for people to travel across the state.

One of the many products shipped by Houston railroads was (and is) cotton.

The first railroad line in the state was the Buffalo Bayou, Brazos & Colorado. It started running, from what is now part of Houston, in 1853. Within eight years, the growing city had five railroad lines stretching 50 to 100 miles in various directions. A major railroad line, the Houston & Texas Central, began in the city and went northward. By 1873 the line reached all the way from the Gulf of Mexico to the Oklahoma border.

Today nearly two million people live in Houston, making it the fourth largest city in the United States. One reason the city grew so fast is that it constantly improved its way of shipping goods, beginning with the railroad. From oceangoing ships to rocket ships, Houston continued to use new methods of transportation. This helped Houston become an important trading center of the Southwest.

At one time, the only building in Houston was a log cabin. Today downtown Houston contains many tall skyscrapers.

The people who work at the Johnson Space Center help to launch space shuttles.

Houston became a national seaport by building the 51-mile Houston Ship Channel that linked the city to the Gulf of Mexico. When the automobile was invented, the city constructed highways that linked Houston to the rest of Texas. When jet air travel arrived, the city built two large airports that linked Houston to much of the world. Even space travel helped the development of the city, for Houston is home to the Johnson Space Center, the home of NASA's Mission Control. And it all began with the railroad!

3 Making Tracks and Towns

Where the railroad went, a town soon followed, whether it was in North Dakota, Nebraska, or New Mexico. The U.S. government wanted the railroads to keep laying track, so it offered lands and loans to railroad companies. If a company was willing to, it could build miles of tracks and receive a plot of land for each mile along the route. The railroads could then sell this land to new settlers who would create towns and villages close to the tracks.

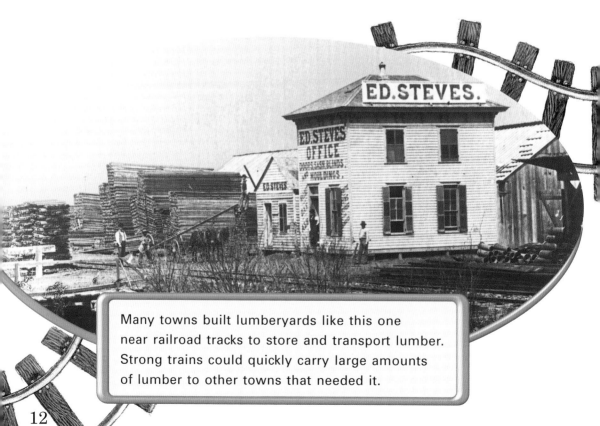

Many towns built lumberyards like this one near railroad tracks to store and transport lumber. Strong trains could quickly carry large amounts of lumber to other towns that needed it.

People in Texas in 1907 wanted to live near railroad tracks so that they could ship and receive goods easily and travel to other places quickly.

The railroad was a better way to move people and products easily and more quickly around the huge state of Texas. For instance, in December 1854, when a person traveled by stagecoach from Houston to a town called Hockley, the 35-mile trip took more than a day. Three years later, a traveler could make that same trip aboard the Houston & Texas Central Railroad. This time it would take just one hour and forty minutes.

Because many Texas towns were created by the railroad, they were often named for people who had something to do with the railroad. The towns of George West and Tom Bean, for example, were named for men who gave land to build towns along the tracks. The community of Ben Arnold was named for a three-year-old girl who traveled on the first train to arrive in town. Cushing and Boyd were last names of men who ran railroads, and Penelope was the first name of a railroad president's daughter. Then there's Valentine, Texas, which was named when the railroad-building crew reached the area on Valentine's Day, February 14, 1882.

The railroad affected the names of many Texas towns, such as Penelope, Texas.

Name that Train!

The Texas Central Railroad was known as the Lone Star Line. Here are some other interesting railroad nicknames:

ABC	Atlanta, Birmingham and Coast Railroad
MOP	Missouri Pacific Railroad
Three C Route	Charleston, Cincinnati and Chicago Railroad
The Katy Route	Missouri-Kansas-Texas Railroad
Corn Belt Route	Chicago Great Western Railroad
Deep Water Route	Gulf, Florida & Alabama Railroad
Route of the Flying Crow	Kansas City Southern Railroad
The Fishing Line	Grand Rapids & Indiana Railroad
Line of the Minute Man	Boston and Maine Railroad

4 Next Stop . . . Waco!

The city of Waco, on the shores of the Brazos River, was known as a place where people could rest while going from one place to another. Some of these people were pioneers heading west, while others were cattle drivers passing through town along the famous Chisholm Trail.

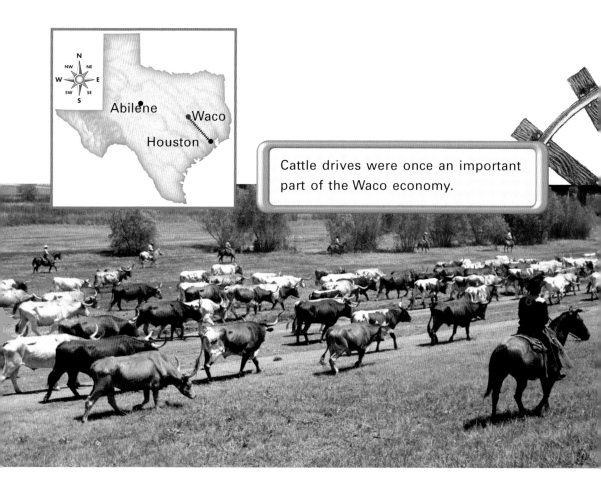

Cattle drives were once an important part of the Waco economy.

The railroad helped turn Waco into a large city with many colorful buildings.

But after the Waco and Northwestern Railroad came to Waco, the town changed from a stopping point to a shipping point. In fact, the railroad helped Waco become an important center for the cotton industry, an industry that's still important to the economy of Texas.

Three different developments helped Texas to produce more cotton than any other state. First, in 1873, Joseph Glidden invented barbed wire. Farmers could use barbed wire to fence in their cotton fields and keep straying cattle and sheep from coming in to trample their crops. Second, farm equipment, such as a plow that broke up the thick sod and hard ground and special machines that helped harvest and bale the cotton, became available to farmers. And last, freight trains were able to bring heavy loads of cotton to markets all across the country much faster than earlier forms of transportation could.

With barbed wire to protect their fields from cattle, farmers could grow more cotton.

By 1884 three railroads ran through Waco, 12,000 people lived there, and nearly 50,000 bales of cotton had been shipped from the city. Because Waco became one of the most important cotton markets in the South, the city held an annual Cotton Palace fair, which attracted an amazing crowd of 117,208 people in one day in 1923. Today nearly that many people call Waco home, as well as close to 250 businesses that produce everything from tires and glass to sporting goods and furniture.

Harvesting machines helped workers pick large amounts of cotton quickly, and compresses smashed air out of cotton bales to make them smaller and easier to stack.

5 Hard Work and Celebration

Building the early railroads was difficult, disagreeable, and dangerous work. It took thousands of people to complete a rail line, often through harsh wilderness. Most of the workers were from other countries, especially China and Ireland. However, many freed slaves and former soldiers helped, too. The railroad crews built bridges over rivers, cleared trees as tall as buildings, and carved tunnels through rock-hard mountains.

Like these workers, thousands of people shared the difficult task of building the railroads.

The Texas Express Tattler

★

April 28, 1869

Railroad Record Set

The crew building the Central Pacific railroad performed an amazing feat today! Two railroad executives wondered whether it was possible for workers to lay 10 miles of track in 1 day and challenged their workers to do just that. After only 12 hours, the crew of thousands had built 10 miles and 56 feet of track, breaking the old 1-day record by 2 miles. That's 24½ feet of track every 20 seconds!

Towns often celebrated the arrival of the railroad, for the residents knew that the hard work would help their communities grow and prosper. When the first train arrived in Waco in 1872, it was met by 3,000 cheering citizens and a band. Waco's oldest citizen drove the final spike, or large nail, into the tracks before the train pulled up. And years later in 1905, when the tracks reached a Texas settlement called Munz, 2,000 people attended a celebration that included a town picnic and a baseball game.

This float was built in St. Paul, Minnesota, to celebrate the completion of the Great Northern Railroad in the summer of 1893.

Lines of both transportation and communication stretched across the United States. Soon telegraph machines could be used to send messages back and forth between the East and the West.

Of course, the biggest party was held when the first transcontinental railroad was completed. This connected the eastern United States to the western United States. And another new invention, the telegraph, was involved. The telegraph uses electricity to carry messages through wire. Telegraph poles had been built along the railroad tracks. When the railroad was completed, a man called a telegrapher operated the telegraph machine to send the news from coast to coast. This way the whole nation could celebrate—and it did! The Liberty Bell rang in Philadelphia, more than 200 cannons were fired in San Francisco, and Chicago held its biggest parade of the century.

The tracks of the Texas & Pacific Railway (T&P) run right through the center of Abilene, Texas, and if it weren't for the railroad, the city wouldn't even exist. When the T&P wanted to extend its line through the western part of Texas, a group of businessmen decided to have the tracks cross their land. The T&P agreed and tracks were constructed 13 miles north of Buffalo Gap, the county seat. A new town called Abilene grew in this spot.

The county seat is the town where leaders of the county meet to discuss important issues.

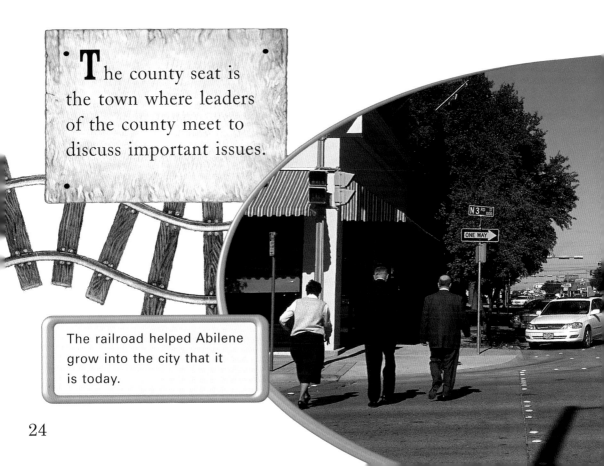

The railroad helped Abilene grow into the city that it is today.

Abilene was named after Abilene, Kansas, which was the end of many cattle drives from Texas before the railroads made tracks through the western central part of the state. From Kansas the cattle were carried along already-established railroad lines. But the arrival of the T&P allowed this lonely new town in the Lone Star state to become an important railroad center of its own. The railroad companies began to call Abilene the "Future Great City of West Texas."

Although the railroad helped to create Abilene, the city's leaders knew that this rough frontier town still had a long way to go before it actually became the "Future Great City." They built schools and churches, and when Abilene was only three years old, its leaders began holding fairs to show off what their farms produced. And, of course, the city's leaders asked that more railroad connections be built through town.

The people of Abilene pass daily by the T&P Railroad Station.

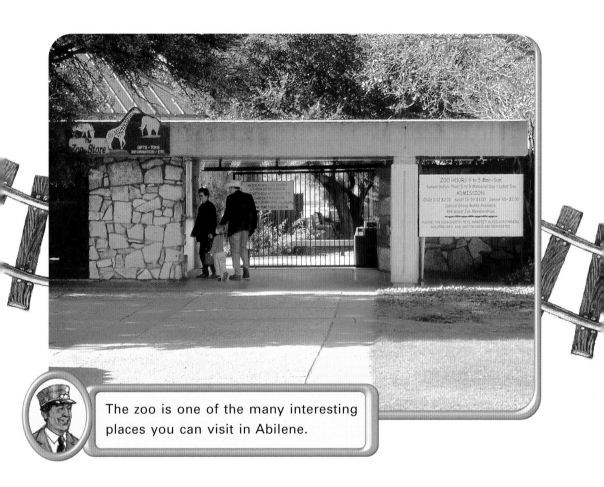

The zoo is one of the many interesting places you can visit in Abilene.

Today with more than 115,000 residents, Abilene is indeed a busy city. It has a community theater, a zoo, and art, history, and children's museums. However, raising cattle is still important to the people of Abilene. Each year it is the site of a huge cattle show and sale.

7 End of an Era

How important the railroad was to Texas can also be seen in the towns that didn't prosper or that disappeared entirely. Do you remember Buffalo Gap, the county seat 13 miles south of Abilene? The year before the railroad helped build up Abilene, Buffalo Gap was home to 1,200 residents. But because people wanted to live near the tracks where Abilene was established, Buffalo Gap's population was down to 300 people within 10 years. Today Buffalo Gap's main attraction is a group of historic buildings that remind visitors of what it once was.

Among the old buildings at Buffalo Gap Historic Village is the first cabin built in the area.

Like Buffalo Gap, the U.S. railroad system is no longer what it used to be. In the twentieth century, it was replaced by other forms of transportation. Automobiles, trucks, buses, and finally airplanes began carrying the people and the cargo once carried by trains. Today Texas tops the nation with nearly 300,000 miles of roads and highways. The train is no longer the only speedy way to cross our large nation.

Today trucks carry much of the freight previously carried by the railroads.

The United States, however, still depends heavily on the railroad. In fact, nearly 10,000 freight trains rumble over more than 150,000 miles of track every day. People ride passenger trains all over the country, too. If they want to, Texans can ride the Texas Eagle train north from San Antonio to Chicago or travel from east to west on the Sunset Limited. And people from all the other states can travel to Texas or to any other state they'd like to visit. There's even a passenger train on the East Coast with a loading platform longer than the height of the Sears Tower—the tallest building in the United States!

So long from the Texas Express, but keep an eye out for a railroad near you!

If you take one of these trains, you can eat, sleep, look at beautiful scenery, and even watch movies!

New Methods
of Transportation

First U.S. railroad
model is
demonstrated. **1825**

First transcontinental
railroad is finished. **1869**

First U.S.
gasoline-powered
automobile is built. **1893**

First manned
airplane is flown. **1903**

An act to create
an interstate highway
system is passed by
the U.S. Congress. **1956**

Boeing 707 **1958**
passenger jets are
first used in the
United States.

Almost 4 million **1993**
miles of highways
spread across the
United States.

1800

1850

1900

1950

2000

Transportation
Events in Texas

Texas' first railroad—
the Buffalo Bayou,
Brazos & Colorado—
1853 begins running.

Houston & Texas
Central Railway creates
1873 the first railroad track
connecting Texas to
St. Louis and the East.

1891 Railroad Commission
forms to make rules for
the operation of Texas
railroads.

A portion of what
became Texas's first
interstate highway
1952 opens in Houston.

Union Station in Dallas
closes from lack of use.
1969

Trains begin bringing
1973 passengers to Union
Station once again.

The train Texas Eagle
2000 begins running daily
trains between San
Antonio and Chicago.

Index

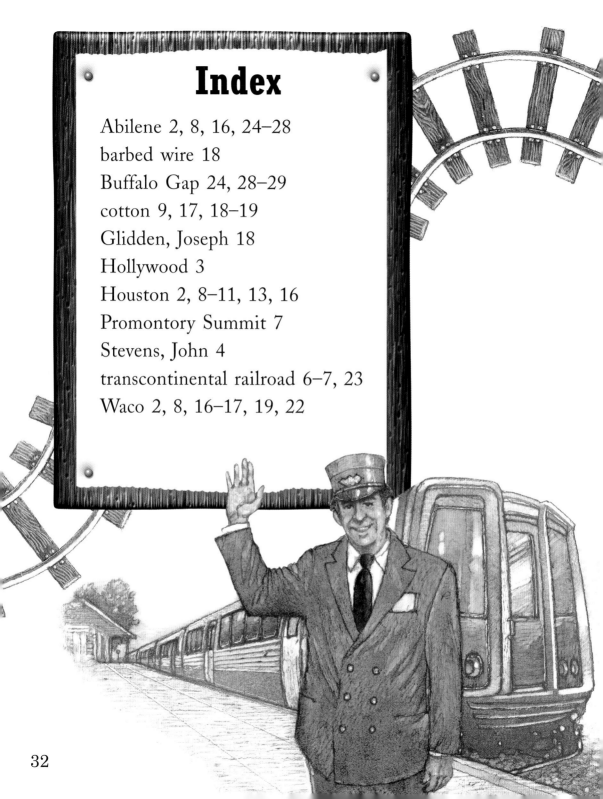